Comments

C.B. says, "Excellent read for teenagers. This makes sex education interesting, yet informative."

M.G. says, "The basketball story would be great for 9th graders."

J.E. says, "Teaches a lesson in a non-threatening way."

J.R. says, "This is a tongue-in-cheek work, but the t-shirt slogans are entertaining."

A.M. says, "Excellent."

J.K. says, "Enlightening."

R.C. says, "It is laugh out-loud funny."

L.B. says, "A fresh, new idea for using with kids about this sensitive topic."

J.B. says, "A titillating read!!!"

B.Q. says, "A unique way to educate the masses, humor the reader, and teach a valuable lesson."

THREE little STORIES

by

I. M. But Naked

ISBN 978-0-6151-8022-9

DEDICATED TO MY PARKING PLACE

LITTLE JOE

Once upon a time, God brought into the world Little Joe. Little Joe was born on the same day as I, in the same hospital, and at exactly the same time.

We were neighbors. In fact, we grew up together, and I often played with him. We lived in the same places, as our dad was in the Army, assigned to many places around the world.

We went to the same schools together and took the same classes. We could have been teachers' pets, but we kept to ourselves. No matter how I longed "that" particular teacher to pet my buddy, she never would. Little Joe was so lonely.

Little Joe

Little Joe and I played in the same sports, to have included football. I remember during the physical when the doctor had to hold Joe to see if he was O.K. Indeed, he was all right and was allowed to play football with me. Lucky for him, though, I protected his neck from harm.

I was involved in an accident one summer. Though Little Joe didn't get hurt, he was saddened because I ended up in the hospital. As he had no one to play with him, Little Joe stayed with me during my ordeal.

Little Joe tried to convince the cute nurses to play with him, or at least kiss him to make him feel better. But none ever did. Little Joe was so lonely.

Injured Little Joe

After a month, I was released from the hospital. Little Joe was so, so happy. He wanted to show his excitement, but he knew I frowned upon such public display. So we hung out privately as we did before the accident. While continuing in school studying the curriculum required, we started enjoying the beauty of the girls.

Little Joe Notices Girls

I remember "that" particular teacher, who was the best-looking female in the school. Little Joe ached and strained when I gazed upon her, but he never caused any problems in class. I know, maybe Little Joe should have acted up, especially in her class, because he would have been beaten. Little Joe was growing up.

Little Joe didn't like goofing off, but he dreamed about what would have happened:

Little Joe would have his neck in the open, as he would have been spanked, and spanked terribly. When this occurs, he gets flustered and tense with bulging veins and turning red, almost purple. And if the spanking wouldn't cease, he would blow his cool. (Believe me! You wouldn't want Little Joe to blow up. He makes such a mess, an animal, when stroked the right way.)

Eventually, Little Joe would settle down for the next succession of events, as "that" particular teacher would kiss him on his forehead.

But with his luck, Little Joe would have had to clean up the mess, for he was UNLUCKY and lonely.

Well, that never happened.

Little Joe and I started going to church. It is wonderful what God and the Bible say about life, living, and eternal salvation. Little Joe and I were baptized together; we asked for it that way.

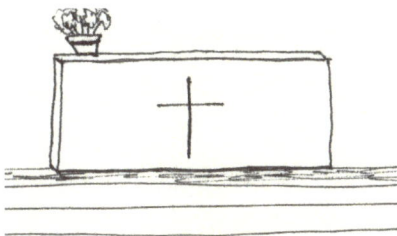

Little Joe Goes to Church

We only hope others find the love and joy of God that Little Joe and I have found. Never again will either of us fear the eternal flame, for HELL would upset us both.

Live On! Devil Be Gone!

We try; we do our best. Little Joe now wants more than ever to visit someone's home. Indeed, he is looking for a home in which to belong. He wants a household, a family, and a life purpose. It's funny; he never asked me how I felt. He just assumed I would go along.

He has tried several houses, and he has had to pay admission a few times. He most times had an umbrella to protect himself from leaky roofs some houses had, as well, as the wet, dark and deep caves in which some houses existed.

Being without an umbrella or hat, and prior to the onset of rain, Little Joe many times found himself out in the light and upon dry land. It was there where he cried rivers of joy for avoiding the inevitable monsoons of the jungle. Sometimes, though, Little Joe got drenched. Little Joe was never satisfied with what he saw and experienced. He was so lonely.

I must look after Little Joe, as he wants to go into unknown places where sickness, illness and disease may lurk. I stop him before he gets into serious trouble. At times, I need to squeeze him back into submission. He has lost his heated cool on me on occasion. Even after a permanent residency is found, Little Joe's badness will continue to get scolding.

Little Joe with Umbrella

I'm happy, too, that my buddy never had the desire to be with some other john. Little Joe knew that temptation and indulgence otherwise was corrupt and potentially fatal. I know he knows that we are life-long friends. Little Joe always made sure he wasn't destined for a dead-end alley. Little Joe wrote a poem about this very situation:

Head

It is the flow of blood to the head
That causes it to become red
It wants then only to go to bed
But not with Ted nor an Ed
It would rather be dead
Than with diseases to live with and dread
For it has been said
And many times read
Unless it's with a gal nicknamed "Fred"
It's quite dangerous the clothes to shed
And unzip that little piece of lead

Little Joe and I searched the world over and found nothing. I remember one time a girl whom I met almost choked Little Joe to death. Although she handled him so badly he couldn't even spit, Little Joe could still stand erect and salute. Little Joe was so lonely.

Then one day, I met someone I thought would be perfect for my and Little Joe's predicament. I shared with her, and Little Joe strained to hear the sweet words whispered into my ears.

I told her of Little Joe and how we looked after each other's best interests. I told her we came together as a complete solid unit and set, a work of God's craft.

Together, Little Joe and I found refuge in her house. She loved and cared for us both. And Little Joe was quick to notice the kiss upon my lips when she offered permanent residency. He shot up eager for the same tender (gulp) kiss that I enjoyed. She often obliged, as she would kiss and caress him.

Little Joe was ever so grateful to God for choosing such a person for a HOME. He wanted natural mountains, with a valley filled with bushes overlooking the house.

Little Joe was defiantly resolved to have a direct driveway into the garage of the house, which would have room for expansion, possibly to include a nursery.

Now, I'm teaching Little Joe how to drive. Before hitting the streets, he must know how to drive and to drive and to drive again into the garage. If Little Joe remembers to keep the driving practice at home and not at other houses, then we will always have a place to park.

Little Joe at Home
The End

Other Favorite Photos

Use one!

Dope? Nope!

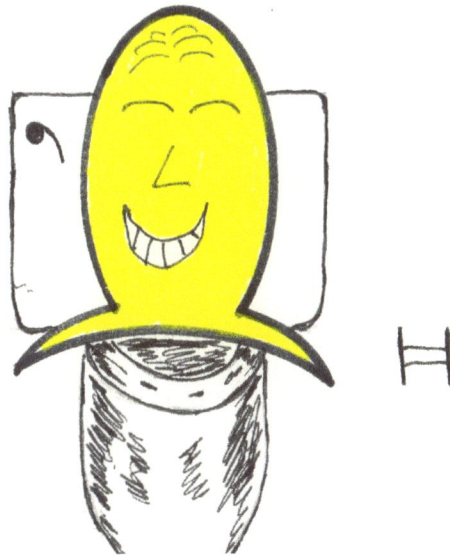

Hun, where's the paper?

All animals have rights...to be grilled.

Another Photo

Kondoms, The Connection Protection

Favorite T-shirts

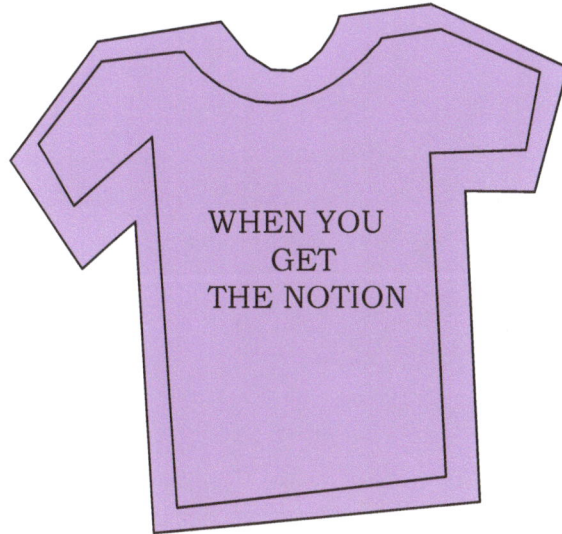

MOTION

WHEN YOU
GET
THE NOTION

LOVERS THREE

LEAVE BE

LOVERS TWO

WILL DO

17

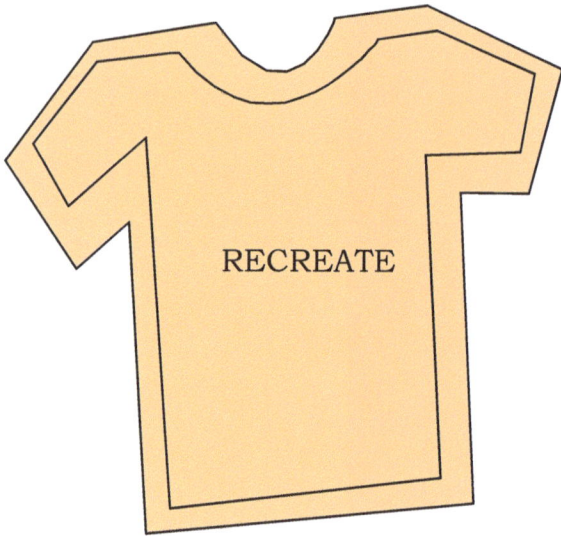

RECREATE

DON'T
PROCREATE

DO FEER

TOO   MUCH

BEER

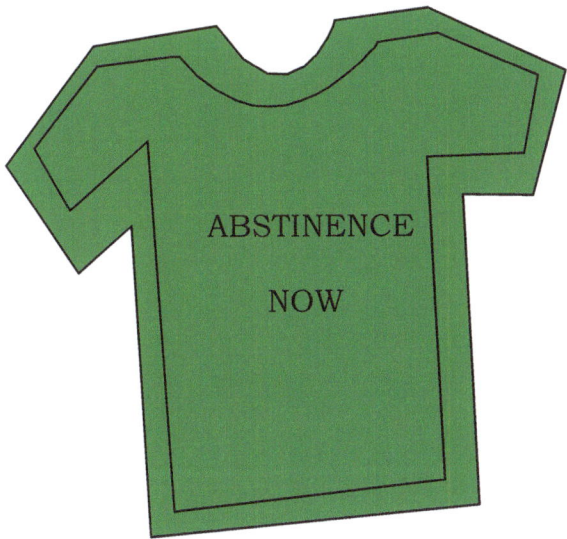

ABSTINENCE

NOW

LATER--

WOW!

HEY
SPORT!

DON'T
ABORT!

USE

ONE !

WHEN YOU

HAVE FUN!

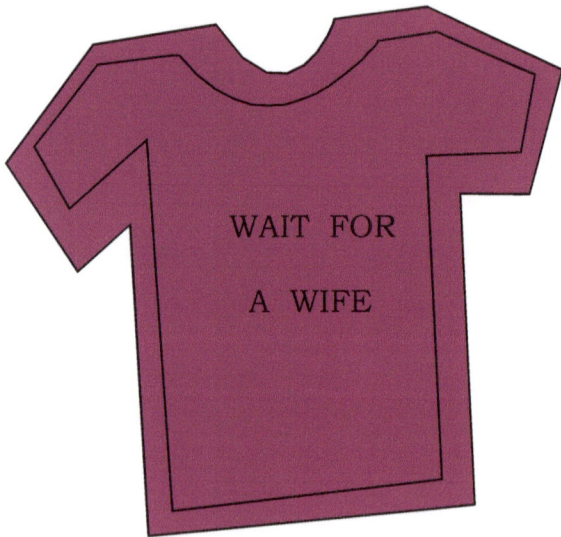

WAIT FOR

A WIFE

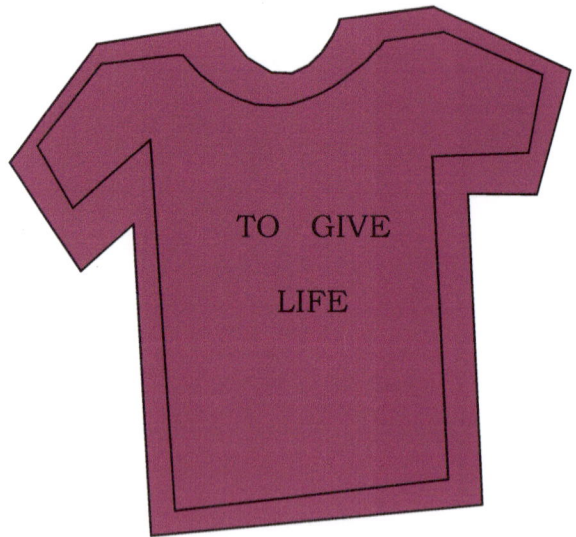

TO GIVE

LIFE

BE

RECEPTIVE

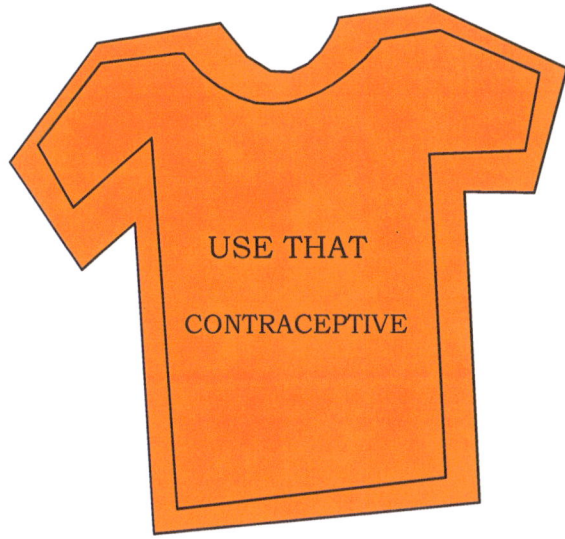

USE THAT

CONTRACEPTIVE

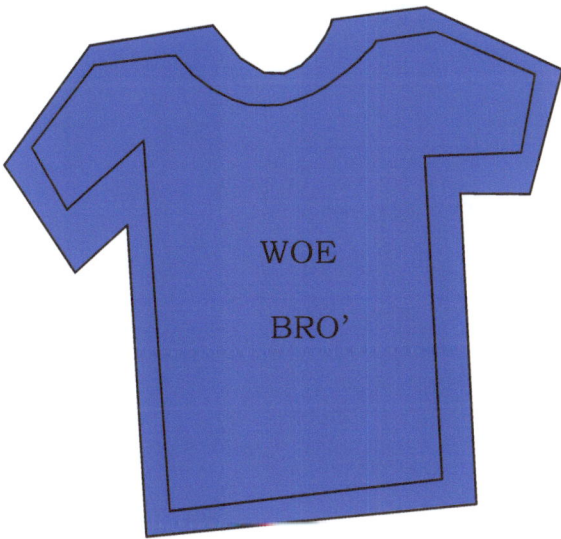

WOE

BRO'

DON'T

SOW

GIVE AN

INKLING

COVER

THE DINKLING

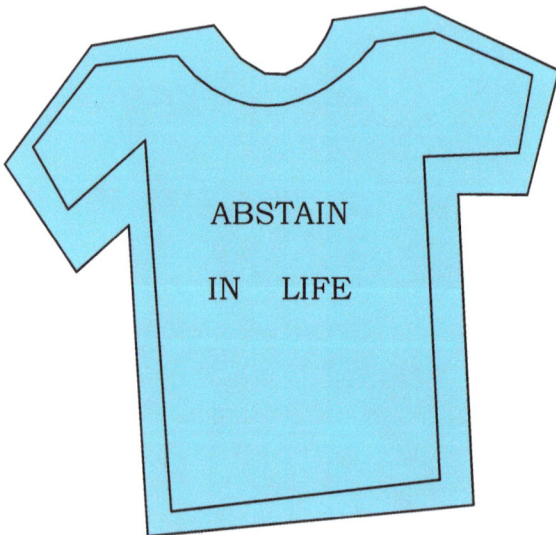

ABSTAIN

IN   LIFE

TO HELP

SUSTAIN

LIFE

GOT THE

URGIN'?

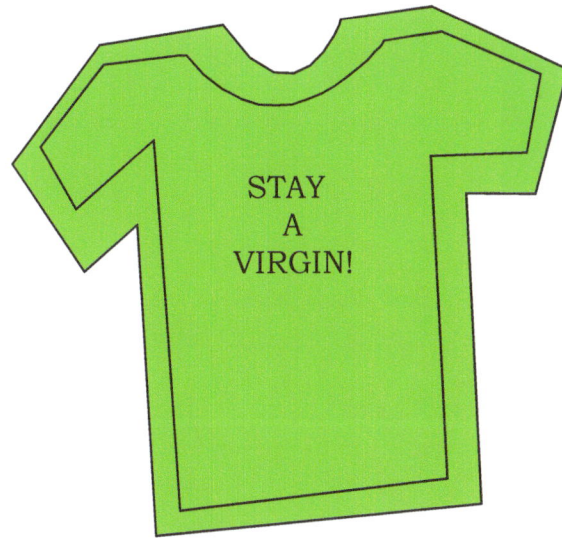

STAY
A
VIRGIN!

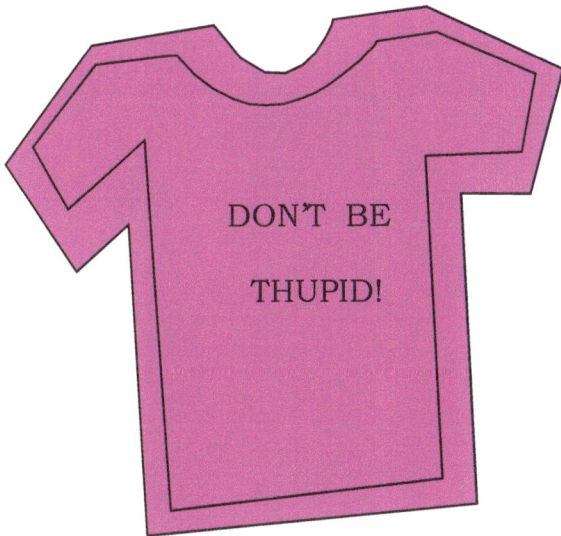

DON'T BE

THUPID!

DON'T
DRINK
AND
DRIVE!

HEY

FLUBBER!

USE A

RUBBER!

HAVE FUN

NOT A SON

USE IT

WHEN YOU

DO IT

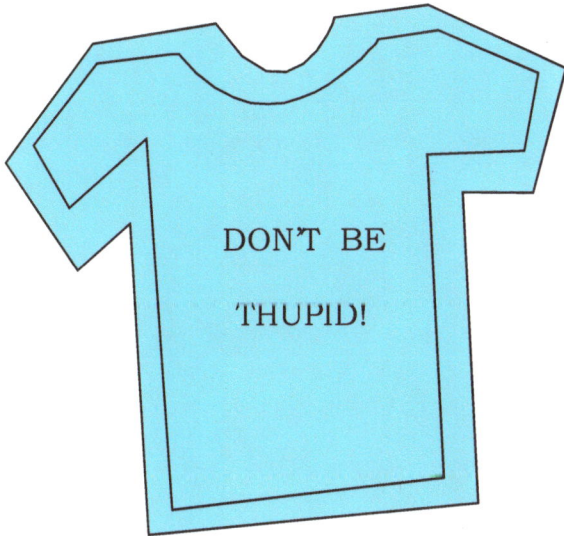

DON'T BE

THUPID!

USE ONE!

DEDICATED TO THE ONE WHO LOOKS AT ME FOR WHAT I CAN BECOME

Ride the Horsey

There once lived a little family in a little house. They lived in a little city in a little state on God's little earth. The family lived off the land onto which God watered, and abundant fruits and vegetables grew on the land. The little family consisted of a father, a mother, a little son, and a littler daughter. The family also had a little dog.

Like looking at uncultivated rich soil and seeing great potential, the family looked at not what they were, but rather at what they could become – a strong, caring and loving family unit.

The little family had respect amongst themselves, for they had made the trek to the little city from faraway. They had little worries and little cares. Much can be learned from the little family, which lived in God's little world.

Nature provided the necessary products with which to survive. Little trees yielded nuts and apples eaten by the family, and little vines nurtured by God produced ample beans, grapes, strawberries, black currants, and other berries. The rich ground, when properly sown, provided seasoned soil in which to grow cabbage, potatoes, radishes, and various other little grains. Indeed, God's land gave much.

But nature and God also provided woman who kept the little house together. God ordained her to do so, for He gave her special gifts. Though it speaks of man's needing companionship, man's departing from his mother and clinging and becoming one with his wife, the Bible does not mention the plight of woman. Was she left uncared for by God? While man has sought refuge since Eve, what and where was woman to seek? Therefore, strength, courage, and wisdom were God's blessings to woman.

It was this woman, younger, who, years earlier, looked at the man for what he could, and had become – a loving and caring husband, as well as a committed father of their two little children. Too often people overlook the potential of others, caught up in immediate self-gratification, looking only at physical characteristics and ignoring (un-) or under-developed qualities.

The woman lovingly cared for the little family of hers. From cleaning up after breakfast, she cooked, sewed and tidied up during the course of the day. She also took care of their little dog. She was a hard little worker.

And when the rest of the family returned home each afternoon, they were grateful to the little woman who toiled the day through cleaning up little bedrooms, sewing up and knitting little holes, and cooking up a wonderful little dinner using God's natural little products.

After dinner, the family always worked together in washing up the dinner table and dishes. Everyone, including the little worker who laboured all day in the little house, shared in the responsibilities.

Once the little family finished up the table and dishes, it was time for their assigned little chores to be done. The little son and the littler daughter rotated between taking out the trash and walking and feeding the little dog. All had a duty to keep this a happy little family.

Each child then had to complete their little homework assignments prior to watching television or joining any family entertainment in the living room of their little house. When necessary, the little woman also assisted with questions the little son and littler daughter had about the homework lessons, for she was completely committed to her little learning family.

As night grew darker in the little city in which the family lived, the little son and littler daughter emerged from their little bedrooms to join their parents in the living room of their little house. Since the children had finished all their little chores and homework assignments, it was still early for them to watch a little television before going to bed.

Tired and sleepy, the father gave the little son the time he wanted him and his little sister to be in bed. The parents then retreated to their little bedroom. The children watched a little television until the designated time, which often fell a little before the late news.

One night, though, a little special show interrupted the regular program. Wanting to watch it, as he was a little interested, the little son saw that his little sister dozed off, so he decided to help her to bed.

The little son first helped his sister to her little bed. And after giving her a little peck of a goodnight kiss, the little son then departed the bedroom, closing the door as he left.

It happened while he walked down the hallway of the little house. The little son heard funny sounds coming from his parent's bedroom. The little son stepped closer, ever so quietly, so as to not disturb and interrupt whatever caused the noise. Quietly and attentively the son listened to some of the conversation coming from the little bedroom of his parents.

"Ride the horsey?" a voice asked.

"Sure!" was the reply, though muffled as it was. Squeaking noises could also be heard coming from the bedroom.

"Ride that horsey! Oh, ride it, baby!" the little son also barely detected, as if an attempt was made to keep down the volume.

"Whoopee. Hee haw," yelped someone. The noises went on for several moments.

"Change saddles?" said by one whom the son determined was his father.

"Sure. It is my turn to ride the horsey. Ready?" asked the mother.

The little worker who laboured the whole day, the one who cooked the little dinner, washed clothes, and tidied up little bedrooms; the teacher who assisted the children with homework assignments; and the woman whom God ordained with strength, courage, and wisdom, for her, this was her refuge.

"I love you," was the final statement the little son heard before he was overtaken by an unexpected cough.

"Who's there? Is that you, son?" asked the father. Only thing heard was the pitter-patter of little feet down the hallway. "I hope he learned something."

The son reached his bedroom door and quickly, but quietly, entered and raced to get in under the sheets of his bed. He indeed learned that the woman, his mother, who cares and loves this little family, received her just reward this night. This reward, he learned, was his father's little duty to keep the family a happy one.

Furthermore, the little son learned that in this country, what happens in the bedroom is no one else's business save those involved. The little son also learned his parents loved each other greatly, just as they loved him and his sister.

For the life of him, though, the little son didn't remember his parents buying a pony or horse, real or mechanical, for it surely would have been a family entertainment piece. "If my parents did get a horsey," wondered the little son, "why in the world was it in the bedroom?"

So went the story of the little family, the one with big love, living in their little house in a little city in God's wonderful little world.

The End

DEDICATED TO THOSE INVOLVED IN THE BATTLES OF SEXUAL
PROTECTION, EDUCATION AND INOCULATION

The Kondoms

Heard coming from a television set: "We interrupt the regular program to bring you this little special show!!"

"Now playing, the greatest basketball teams ever to have been assembled in one place at one time in a battle to the finish, a winners-take-all confrontation. It is the Game of the Century: The Kondoms verses the VD's.

"Introducing first, a team composed of various subjects present in every walk of life and from various parts of the world. An international team consisting of magnified, yet individual traits, characteristics and abilities, are represented here. It is truly a horrible team when in combat together, but controlled and neutralized when its horrors are prevented separately.

"This team was formed, for the most part, from negligence and carelessness of individuals. Perhaps uninformed! Perhaps uneducated! Perhaps laziness caused this demise! Whatever the reason, this team has caused death, destruction, and downfall of individuals, families, and institutions. This team has swept the world with its on-slaught of wicked power. If only we could learn. Now the headliners of one of the teams playing today, the VD's."

From part unknown, though it's thought Europe, is Vaginal Warts. Wearing Number 1, "VW," nicknamed "Bug," this little booger will foul in all the wrong places. It'll be a threat to the satisfaction of foreplay for that matter. It hinders entrance to the keyhole area and makes shooting an unrealistic goal.

From South America, and nicknamed "Chicken Man," wearing Number 2, Chlamydia is a threat to coming into the keyhole area, as well. Entry by jump shot or set shot is potentially hazardous and therefore should not be attempted without adequate team coverage.

Like all the VD's, Syphilis, of the Adriatic, is also a pain. Wearing Number 5, Syphilis gets into your blood and bodily fluids, causing havoc and eventual poor outcome. It stays in your system for months, often years, as you cannot rid yourself of this wickedness. Syphilis can enter the body by simple kiss, or by attack to cuts and open sores. The only remedy is by letting "The Doctor" handle it. Otherwise, further medical participation off court may be required.

Wearing Number 3, a giant of a sickness, Gonorrhea, of Southeast Asia, infects your vital organs. A big violator of double dribbling, its presence can be discovered prior to ball transfer, though it may not be known by the one to whom the ball is passed. Neglect by team officials to scout the opposition could result in disaster.

Finally, wearing Number 4, it is even a threat while being double-teamed. The VD's main star seems to be a newcomer, though possibly by name only. No one knows from where it comes. Many believe Africa, but many others believe it has always been around. Left unprotected, it develops from the entry by an invisible sidekick, HIV.

HIV infection is the first stage of this offensive attack, getting into the immune system and destroying white blood cells. Over time, while playing or playing around, the frightful forecourt or backcourt attack sets in to deliver the deathblow to its victims. It is presumed all have lost (died) at the beating the invisible HIV and this star do to the opposing sides.

With its invisible sidekick helping with hook shots and slam-dunks, and in what could be a technical foul, this monster is doubly difficult to cover and neutralize. It produces a one extra player advantage in today's game. The VD's main star of the century: A.I.D.S.

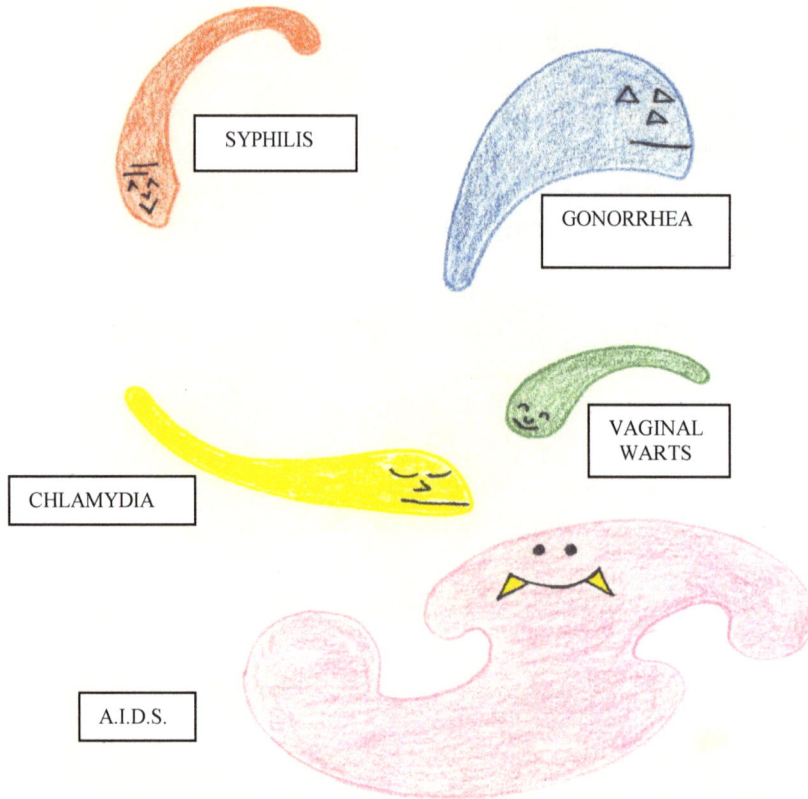

SYPHILIS

GONORRHEA

CHLAMYDIA

VAGINAL WARTS

A.I.D.S.

Don't be fooled by their smiles. They are a vicious group.

The task may seem impossible, but the Kondoms have put their heads together and have come up with a game plan to stop the VD's from attacking and subjecting others to pain, suffering, and possible death, while on the court of life.

Now we go courtside, where our commentator, Larry, is standing by with the opposing team of this Game of the Century, The Kondoms.

"Thank you, Bob. Thank you, ladies and gentlemen, for joining us for this evening's game, indeed, today's championship round. Like a seesaw battle, some will be lost and some will be won. But one thing for sure, the fight must continue.

"The Kondoms have been up all night, warming up for this game. It is a serious matter. It is a matter of life and death. And the Kondoms are out to prove their point: that with them, the VD's are neutralized and their tortures stopped. The Kondoms are an inspirational source of power, strength, and defense, as they play continuously in the role of "Protector."

"Let's turn to another side of the Kondoms. The Kondoms recently recorded a hit rap song through their label, *Come Again.*

Let's listen to it now. It's called *"VD Rap Song:"*

Up, down, shake, and stop,
We're out to halt that loving bop.
We're Meat, Stinky, Dick and Hairy,
We've also got the Doctor fairy.
You say you're gonna pop that cherry,
Ain't gonna be a funkin' fairy.
But what happens when you're in,
Deep, deep, deep in skin?
Have you ever thought,
"What about if I caught,
A, B, C through Z's,
What about that V disease?"
But we are here today,
And to you got this to say:
You don't have to have a fit,
But unsafe sex's a bottomless pit.
Venereal D of all sorts,
First of all is Vaginal Warts.
As you wonder why,
Do know V D also comes from a guy.
Number Two
Is after you.
Now we have Chlamydia.
Oh no! Here comes that mutha!
Next up is Number Three.
Makes you hurt when you pee.
Here's our man, he's up to say,
"Use protection fan, and keep V D at bay."
Also says, "Listen to me all of yah;
We'll not spread Gonorrhea."
Next up, too, is no fun,
As our song is not yet done.

If you'll listen to us,
We're out to stop that Syphilis.
Final up is Number Four.
Folks, it's killing more and more.
Makes no difference, big or small,
A-I-D-S could kill us all.
Although AIDS wears Number Four,
It don't gotta kill any more.
Now you're thinking about Five.
Ponder this before you dive:
Acquired Immune Deficiency Syndrome
Ain't no match with a healthy Kondom.
So go ahead and spank your monkey,
No V D is really funky.
On top of these we will be
Stopping the spread of H-I-V.
You may say we're a joker,
Consider this before you poke her:
No more cram, bam, and thank you, Ma'm.
Listen here to slam your ham.
Next time you're in that loving stupor,
Go with Kondoms, because they are super!

During recruiting tryout week, encouragement is stressed to all newcomers that it could be risky to get to the basket area for a shot without veteran Kondom support. Doing so without coverage could deliver unwanted additional responsibility or it could lead to downfall.

All regular visitors for tryout are accompanied by a Kondom, as the team already knows the habits and maneuvers the Kondoms are to face this evening. Satisfaction otherwise could be very, very dangerous. However, if a participant has a preferred teammate, and if both have been screened for compatibility, then the coach (God) may give permission for tryout and practice with that partner.

Now introducing the Kondoms, the only force which can whip the VD's before they happen:

Playing guard, the local, tobacco-chewing native, nicknamed "Meat," is Big Red. When asked what school he attended, all Big Red says is "Up Urs." Meat wears a headband and a traditional strand of hair on his otherwise baldhead.

Great at defense, Meat is tough and hard to get around. Short, but stocky, Meat carries himself well, and he will stuff all holes that open his way. (Must be from his Up Urs days.)

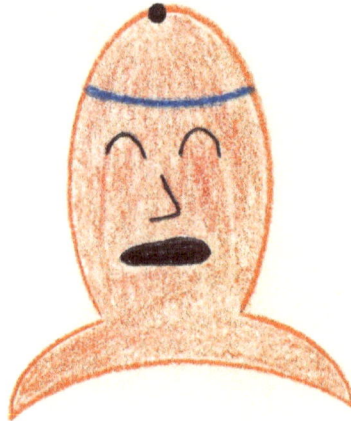

Big Red "Meat"

Also starting is the West Coast Oriental, out of P.U., Richard Wadd. Dick uses his upbringing and flexibility to control all situations. Able to bounce with perfect control two balls at once, Dick can bounce them together or alternately, depending on the position he's in. This will be exciting when he is in the keyhole area to make a shot. He provides any necessary offense for the team.

Richard "Dick" Wadd

Harold "Hairy" Ball, out of T. & C.U., is the primary defensive player. Hairy has lightening-fast hands. When it appears as though he will be scratching that body of his, Hairy will be actually going for the ball with which the VD's wish to score. With his silky-like body, Hairy will be able to slide easily into crevices for proper defensive positioning.

Harold "Hairy" Ball

42

"The Doctor," from the Midwest, is the only transsexual attempting to return to his/ her God-given life. Rozy Palmer is really an example by which to learn. Able to palm two balls with either hand at one time, Rozy is known for his/ her good hands and ball control.

Although he/ she knows how to handle the ball, Rozy still gets rimmed and slammed at least once a game. He/ She is a fired-up player, ready to alleviate any doubts that the Kondoms are a force shameful to be without. Though his/ her specialty is Syphilis, he/ she will run down any V D and make it wish it gulped that last bit of juice left from breakfast in bed.

Rozy "The Doctor" Palmer

Nicknamed "Stinky," Jakov Overhier was a European transplant from Analsia prior to signing and becoming a rising star with that Harlem team. He is a sensation to the Kondoms line-up. Certain to be All-star material, Jakov became available only after the fall of the Iron Curtain.

Jakov is very talented, and playing center, he can shoot from anywhere on the court. He can dribble and drive the ball. Defensively, Jakov can stuff any player's shot, stopping it from entering the felt-like hole. He is by far the tallest on the court tonight.

Jakov "Stinky" Overhier

Analysis

Kondoms		VD's
A	Stuffing Holes	A
A	Teamwork	A
A	Protection	F
F	Offense	A
A	Guarding	F
F	Shooting	A
B	OVERALL	B

The VD's: The VD's will have to overcome the great team strength of the Kondoms. They will have to beat the Meat to possibly have any luck scoring. The grudge between The Doctor and Syphilis will be handled on the court, as the latter wants to the ham past that pink flesh of Rozy's and inflict as much damage as possible. While worthless against a strong defense, the VD's must find holes in the wrong field of protection, the wrong brand play, and the lack of quality the Kondoms might have in development of their game plan.

The Kondoms: On the other side, the Kondoms must watch from all sides, as they are one man down to the HIV. The Kondoms say, "A great defense makes up for a lack of offense." Many analysts, however, say, "A better defense is to not play the game at all now."

The Kondoms must choke the chicken (Chicken Man) and provide adequate protection and coverage to all the other woodies, pointers, rocks, nuts, ding dongs, manhoods, peckers, thingies, dingies, dipsticks, dragons, and one-eyed snow snakes of society. And aside from not getting into the game, if they're left to play their game, the Kondoms should win.

Two good teams! Who wins? Only time will tell. It's all up to us.

Tonight's game, brought to you by a concerned citizen of the world, is being held in a far off location. A location where little exists and life is rare. It is being held in a location where the VD's can do little harm to life.

The sponsor has invited our combatants to come here to battle it out. Uninhibited by weather, environment, and socio-economic conditions, the teams will challenge each other's abilities in this no-holds-barred event.

Here come the VD's onto the court. Why? It's tip-off time. What? They don't need to warm up? Don't they need to stretch out before getting started? I think not.

Welcome to Antarctica! It's summer, yet it's freezing cold. Nothing, but nothing, will stop the Kondoms and the VD's from their appointed destiny.

When you least expect it, the VD's can catch you off guard, when your defenses are down. The VD's actually play neither offense nor defense. They just exist, and they exist because of our own negligence, ignorance, and carelessness. They tear down families, peoples, and institutions with little effort on their part. They overwhelm others when and where people are left unprotected and unguarded. And it's our fault!

We have come here this day to have the Kondoms fight our battle. If you wish to enter life's court, seek proper protection and advise. This is a day of revelation. The day of reckoning has come to this, The Game of the Century.

The End

An After Thought

Obviously, I'm not too concerned about political correctness. For those who think I'm not sensitive enough about social problems, consider these little points:

Little Joe: Have faith.

Ride the Horsey: Learn a Lesson

The Kondoms: Practice safe sex.

Enjoy life, but safely.

www.ingramcontent.com/pod-product-compliance
Lightning Source LLC
Chambersburg PA
CBHW061057090426
42742CB00002B/68